HUMBLE TOM'S BIG TRIP

A Tudor play

Kaye Umansky

For Mo – K.U.

ABOUT THE AUTHOR

Kaye Umansky is best known as the creator of Pongwiffy, the 'witch of dirty habits', whose hilarious antics feature in five books. She is a former teacher with special interests in drama and music, and has written many plays for performance.

HUMBLE TOM'S BIG TRIP

A Tudor play
Kaye Umansky

Illustrated by Chris Mould

an imprint of Hodder Children's Books

Text copyright © Kaye Umansky 2002
Illustrations copyright © Chris Mould 2002

Editor: Gill Munton
Designer: Don Martin

First published in 2002
This edition published in 2003
by Hodder Wayland, an imprint of
Hodder Children's Books

A catalogue record for this book is available
from the British Library.

ISBN: 0 7502 41233

Printed and bound in Hong Kong by Shek Wah Tong

Hodder Children's Books
A division of Hodder Headline Limited
338 Euston Road, London NW1 3BH

INTRODUCTION

The year is 1520, and King Henry VIII has ruled over England for 11 years. He is a handsome, robust giant of a man. A flamboyant character, he has squandered his father's fortune and is more interested in sport, music and dancing than in politics. He is married to Catherine of Aragon, the first of his six wives. Their daughter, Princess Mary, is four years old and already betrothed to the King of France's infant son. These are the so-called "Golden Years" of Henry's reign; he will commit most of his acts of tyranny within the last third.

There are 12 scenes, set in various locations: several rooms in the King's palace at Greenwich, a London street, a hovel in the Kent countryside, the bank of the Thames, and the port of Dover.

The play is intended for reading in class in a single session. There are 32 speaking parts: 15 for girls, 15 for boys and two for either boys or girls. If necessary, one or two of the smaller roles (e.g. the seamstresses) can be omitted. The play can, however, be read in groups of four or five, with some children taking more than one of the smaller roles. This can be arranged on a scene-by-scene basis; the characters who appear in each scene are listed at the beginning.

THE CAST *in order of appearance*

Name	Description	Role
Will	} Narrators	Large
Annie		Large
Henry VIII	The King	Medium
Humble Tom	A shepherd boy	Large
Cardinal Wolsey	Chancellor	Medium
Catherine of Aragon	The Queen	Small

THE CAST

Lady Margaret	} Ladies-in-waiting	Small
Lady Jane		Small
Sarah	} Seamstresses	Small
Hannah		Small
Susan		Small
Princess Mary	Henry's daughter	Small
Nosegay Seller	(Male or female)	Small
Washerwoman		Small
Dairymaid		Small
Woman with Pot		Small
Baker's Boy		Small
Night Soil Collector	(Male)	Small
Barber/Surgeon	(Male)	Small
Candle Seller	(Male or female)	Small
Lord Buckingham	} Noblemen	Small
Lord Rutland		Small
Duke of Sussex		Small
Lady Buckingham	} Noblewomen	Small
Lady Rutland		Small
Duchess of Sussex		Small
Cook	(Male)	Medium
Tom's Mother	A shepherdess	Small
Tom's Father	Her husband	Small
Cutpurse Roger	A thief	Small
Blind Olly	A thief	Small
Dirty Christopher	A thief	Small

7

PROLOGUE

(Will, Annie, Henry VIII, Humble Tom, Cardinal Wolsey)

*A fanfare of trumpets. Lights up on **Will** and **Annie**, the narrators. They remain on stage throughout the play, interjecting and commenting on the action. **Will** is flamboyantly dressed in doublet and hose, with cloak and plumed hat. **Annie** is in a dull Tudor dress.*

Will: Our play begins! Welcome, good fellows all! *(Sweeps off his hat and bows)* Will is my name, and I am your host for the evening. The wench in the drab frock is Annie, here to give you the *female* perspective. From time to time. But not too often, I sincerely hope.

Annie: I can introduce myself, thank you.

Will: Wrong! First mistake. We're in period, remember? These are Tudor times. Men are all-important — right, lads?

*(Off-stage cheers from the **Boys**.
Boos from the **Girls**.)*

Boys: Hooray! Right!

Girls: Booo!

Will: So, on with the play! Settle back and allow me to set the scene.

Annie: Here we go. Long, boring speech coming up.

Will: It is the Year of Our Lord fifteen hundred and twenty. Henry VIII, or Good King Harry, as they call him …

Boys: *(Off-stage)* Long live the King!

Will: Yes, thank you … has reigned over England for eleven years. Has there ever been such a king in all Christendom? Young, handsome, ambitious, athletic, musically talented, a patron of the arts and a lover of good food and hunting. How his loyal subjects love him!

*(Lights up on **Henry VIII**. He is all of the above, and more.)*

Henry VIII: They'd better. Or … kkk!

*(He makes a cut-throat gesture and gives a knowing wink. Lights down on **Henry VIII**.)*

Annie: Excuse me. They don't *all* love him. A lot of people resent his extravagant ways. All those palaces. All those wars. And as for later, when he starts chopping people's heads off and dissolving the monasteries and divorcing his wives when it suits him …

Will: Enough! Such talk is treason. I'm trying to give some historical background here. *(Clears throat and speaks directly to audience)* After several years of war …

Annie: Hold on. Someone's coming.

*(Enter **Humble Tom**. He is barefoot. He wears a mud-splattered smock and a straw hat, and carries a bundle and a shepherd's crook. He trips over a twig.)*

Humble Tom: Oops!

*(He notices **Will** and **Annie** staring at him. He sets down his bundle and gives a humble bow.)*

Humble Tom: Excuse me, Your Lordship. Do this road lead to The Kitchens, The Palace, Greenwich, London Town?

Will: By thunder, am I never to get a word in? A fig on your query, lad. Away with you.

Annie: 'Tis that way. *(Points)*

Humble Tom: Thankee, mistress.

> *(Exit **Humble Tom**, forgetting to take his bundle. He trips over the twig again on his way out.)*

Humble Tom: Ouch!

Will: Who was that?

Annie: Whoever it was, he seems very accident-prone. He left his bundle, look. I wonder what's in it? *(She rummages in the bundle)* Yuck! Cold pottage!

Will: What's pottage?

Annie: A sort of vegetable stew. The poor ate it every day in Tudor times. Want a lump?

Will: Has it got leeks?

Annie: Almost certainly.

Will: No, thanks. To continue. After several years of war, an uneasy peace prevails over England. Cardinal Wolsey, currently chief advisor to King Henry …

Boys: *(Off-stage)* Long live the King!

Will: *(To **Boys**)* Yes, thank you. As I was saying, Cardinal Wolsey has pulled off a bit of a coup …

*(Lights up on **Cardinal Wolsey**, shaking his shoulders and gloating.)*

Cardinal Wolsey: Indeed I have. His Majesty's going to be really pleased with this one. More power, money and influence for me, heh, heh, heh!

*(Lights down on **Cardinal Wolsey**.)*

Will: In order to cement an alliance with the French, clever Wolsey has organised an historic meeting between His Grace King Henry …

Boys: Long live the King!

Will: *(Wincing)* … and King Francis of France. The meeting will take place just outside Calais. There will be two weeks of diplomatic talks …

Annie: As well as feasting and carousing and spending vast amounts of money that could be spent on a decent sewage disposal system. Not to mention the state of the roads.

Will: But you can't blame Henry for wanting to put on a good show. King Francis is one of his biggest rivals.

SCENE 1

(Henry VIII, Cardinal Wolsey, Annie, Will)

*Henry's chambers. Lights up on **Henry VIII**, playing his lute. Enter **Cardinal Wolsey**. Fade music.*

Cardinal Wolsey: Your Majesty! Great news!

Henry VIII: What is it, Wolsey? This had better be good. I'm trying to play "Greensleeves" here. *(Sings)* La la, la la la-la …

Cardinal Wolsey: Sire, I've done it! The meeting is on! Betwixt your majestic self and King Francis of France.

Henry VIII: And that's good, is it?

Cardinal Wolsey: Oh, yes! Imagine it, sire! A dazzling midsummer pageant, full of pomp and splendour. Just outside Calais. *(Craftily)* I hear the wine is very cheap.

Henry VIII: Not just sitting around talking, then?

Cardinal Wolsey: Oh, no, sire. Plenty of jousting, archery, wrestling – all sorts of manly stuff. And the evenings will be given over to dancing, music and feasting.

Henry VIII: Splendid! Excellent opportunity to display our superiority over the French. I've never liked Francis. Might even wrestle him m'self. He's smaller than me.

Cardinal Wolsey: I have cleverly arranged it for July so that we can get away from the stink of the Thames. They can give the Palace a thorough de-lousing while we're away soaking up the French sunshine, ha, ha, ha.

Henry VIII: Ha, ha, ha. Good thinking. I hear that the sweating sickness has broken out again amongst the lower orders. It won't hurt to steer clear of London for a bit.

Cardinal Wolsey: My thoughts precisely.

Henry VIII: *(Suddenly suspicious)* You're quite sure

this will be a *friendly* meeting? I don't trust Francis. No sudden ambushes or surprise breaking out of hostilities? No sneaky poisoning of the wine?

Cardinal Wolsey: Oh, no. And – er – perhaps not *too* much boasting about how good England is compared to France, sire. We need that all-important signature to bind our countries together.

Henry VIII: A plague on false modesty! They're always going on about their food, are they not? We'll throw money at the project! We'll construct vast pavilions, bigger than theirs, and ship 'em piecemeal to France. We'll take our finest archers and swordsmen, and dazzle 'em all with our sporting talents. It'll make a change from fighting wars. Well done, Wolsey. Build yourself a new house or something.

Cardinal Wolsey: Thank you, sire!

*(Lights down on **Henry VIII** and **Cardinal Wolsey**.)*

Annie: *(Sourly)* He does, too. It's called Hampton Court.

Will: Sssh. *I'm* talking. *(To audience)* His Grace is going to great lengths to ensure that the English will outshine the French in the place which will one day be known as the Field of the Cloth of Gold. *(Fanfare)*

Annie: I'm tired of hearing about the King.

16

SCENE *1*

Boys: Long live the K …

Annie: *(To the **Boys**)* Enough, enough! *(To **Will**)* What about Catherine of Aragon? You haven't even mentioned her. We want to hear about the women, don't we?

Girls: *(Off-stage)* Yes! Hooray! Let's hear it for the girls!

Will: You still don't get it, do you? Women don't get a say in how things are run. It will be another three hundred years before you lot get the vote.

Annie: *(Sharply)* Tell that to the queens who rule after Henry.

Will: I'm talking about *ordinary* women. Look, I'm chief narrator. Know your place and kindly do not interrupt.

Girls: *(Off-stage)* Boo!

Annie: Well, I'm sorry, but I must insist. We need a bit of balance. We want to hear about Queen Catherine.

SCENE 2

(Queen Catherine, Lady Margaret, Lady Jane, Annie, Will)

Queen Catherine's chambers. Courtly music. Lights up on Queen Catherine and her ladies-in-waiting, Lady Margaret and Lady Jane.

Queen Catherine: Caramba! I fear my good 'usband tires of me.

Lady Margaret: Oh, no, Your Majesty. Surely not!

Queen Catherine: Why else would 'ee not want me by 'eez side in France? Oh Henery, Henery, what am I doing wrong? *(Sobs)*

Lady Jane: I'm sure he has his reasons, madam.

Queen Catherine: I am eentelligent, accomplished and speerited, and I 'ave exotic Spaneesh accent. All right, so I've failed to provide 'eem weeth a son and heir. But eez that enough reason for 'eem to go off me?

Lady Margaret and Lady Jane: We – e – e – ll …

(The word is left hanging in the air as the lights go down.)

Annie: You see? Don't tell me about Good King Harry.

Boys: *(Off-stage)* Long live the King!

Will: *(Irritably, to the **Boys**)* Oh, be quiet. *(To **Annie**)* All right, point taken. So he didn't treat Queen Catherine too well.

Annie: Or Mary.

Will: What? Who's Mary?

Annie: Poor little Princess Mary. Catherine's only surviving daughter. Betrothed already to the King of France's son, and only four years old. It's common gossip …

19

SCENE 3

(Sarah, Hannah, Susan, Annie, Will)

*A room in the Palace. Lights up on a group of women doing needlework. They are **Sarah**, **Hannah** and **Susan**, the seamstresses. They are working on a flag for the forthcoming journey to France.*

Sarah: *I* hear the Queen isn't going to France.

Hannah: *I* hear she is falling out of the King's favour.

Sarah: Although, of course, there's little Princess Mary to look after. She's only four. Bless!

Sarah, Hannah and Susan: *(Fondly)* Aaaah!

Susan: Poor little lamb. What's His Majesty thinking of? Making a four year-old get engaged to a strange French toddler who can't even speak English.

Hannah: Sssh! Keep your voice down.

Sarah: Susan's right, though. It's a shame. Why can't she make up her own mind? When she's big enough?

Susan: Cruel, I call it.

Hannah: I hear the fiancé's not even on solids yet.

Susan: They should be out in the sun playing, not indoors getting betrothed.

Sarah, Hannah and Susan: Poor little dears.

*(Lights down on **Sarah**, **Hannah** and **Susan**.)*

Annie: You see? I'm not the only one who disapproves. Little Mary should marry who she likes.

Will: That's not the way it's done in royal circles.

Annie: Well, *I* think she should get a chance to say her piece.

Will: And *I* think you've got far too many opinions for a Tudor girl.

Girls: *(Off-stage)* Booooo!

Will: All right, all right! If we must. Let's hear what *Little Mary* has to say.

SCENE 4

(Henry VIII, Mary, Will, Annie)

*The nursery. Lights up on **Henry VIII** and **Mary**.*

Henry VIII: Mary, I know you're a very *little* girl, but I think you should know that I've arranged for you to be married to the son of the King of France when you're older. What do you have to say to that, eh?

Mary: I got a poorly finger. Can I have a pony? I like sugar. Can I have some? Why have I got a Spanish mummy?

*(Lights down on **Henry VIII** and **Mary**.)*

Will: A round of applause for those pearls of wisdom from Mary.

Annie: It would be different if she were a boy. Boys are treated better than girls. Everyone knows King Henry wants a son. He's using his own daughter for political purposes.

Will: Look, I do wish you'd stop interrupting. I've forgotten what I was saying now.

Annie: You were going on about King Henry and the Field of the Cloth of Gold. *(Fanfare)*

Will: Right. Well, it seemed like a good idea at the time. A lot of people were behind him.

Annie: Not the common people …

SCENE 5

(The Nosegay Seller, the Washerwoman,
the Dairymaid, the Woman with Pot,
the Baker's Boy, the Night Soil Collector,
Humble Tom, the Barber/Surgeon,
the Candle Seller, Will)

*A filthy Tudor street. The townsfolk go about
their business. The traders bark their wares.
The **Night Soil Collector** carries a spade. The
Woman with Pot stands at an upstairs window.*

Nosegay Seller: Nosegays! Buy a nosegay, keep the
sweating sickness away!

Washerwoman: Washin'! Who wants their washin'
done? Changed yer beddin' this year, missus?
No? Thought not.

Dairymaid: Milko! Nice fresh milk! Don't risk the
water, 'twill bring you out in lumps.

Woman with Pot: 'Ware below!

*(There is a splashing noise as she empties
her chamberpot.)*

Baker's Boy: Oh, no! Look at that. All over my
bread rolls.

Night Soil Collector: Oi! Watch where yer tippin' it. I gotta clean that up now.

*(Enter **Humble Tom**, with a shepherd's crook but without his bundle. He is dirtier than ever. He walks in something nasty.)*

Humble Tom: Eeeeugh! *(Scrapes his foot with his crook)*

Barber/Surgeon: Haircuts! Want a shave, lad? I can pull yer rotten tooth! Need a crude and risky roadside operation? Tell you what, I'll throw in the leeches free of charge.

Humble Tom: Not today, thank you. *(Looks around)* Oooh. So this is London Town. 'Tis even muckier than the country. *(To **Nosegay Seller**)* Excuse me, friend. Be this the right way for Greenwich?

Nosegay Seller: How should I know? I've never been past the end of the street. Shog off, unless you're buyin' a nosegay.

*(**Humble Tom** lingers, undecided about which way to go. He stands beneath the window as the townsfolk talk.)*

Candle Seller: Have you heard the latest? The King's off to France.

Washerwoman: 'Tis all right for some.

Dairymaid: 'Ow the rich live, eh? Me, I've never been further than my nan's. She lives next door.

Nosegay Seller: Not surprisin', with the state of the roads. Any more rain and we'll all drown in mud.

Candle Seller: The King should do somethin' about it. Rats. Open sewers. Muck everywhere. Nowhere to dump the rubbish.

Baker's Boy: Point of information! There is. It's called the River Thames.

Washerwoman: And what about crime? Someone hooked the clothes off me washin' line again this mornin', can you believe?

Woman with Pot: Another lot coming down! 'Ware below!

*(There is a splashing noise as another chamberpot is emptied from on high. The contents land on **Humble Tom**.)*

Humble Tom: Oh, *figs!*

(Lights down on the street.)

Will: Well, all right, so not everyone approved of the King's plan. But the rich courtiers and noblemen who were to accompany him were full of it.

SCENE 6

**(Lord Buckingham, Lord Rutland,
the Duke of Sussex, Will, Annie)**

The palace grounds. Lights up on
Lord Buckingham, **Lord Rutland** *and*
the **Duke of Sussex***.*

Lord Buckingham: Good morrow, my Lord Rutland.
How fare you?

Lord Rutland: Couldn't be better, sir. His Grace
the King …

Boys: *(Off-stage)* Long live the King!

Lord Rutland: *(Irritably, to the* **Boys***)* Yes, thank you.
As I was saying. His Grace has honoured me
with an invitation to join the royal retinue and
sail with him to France! Hurrah!

Lord Buckingham: Me, too! Hurrah! What glory, eh?
What about you, Sussex?

Duke of Sussex: Naturally, as one of the more *highly*
trusted courtiers, I too will join the King.
(To off-stage **Boys***)* Just don't, all right?

Lord Buckingham: Excellent news! Hurrah!

(They all wave their swords.)

Lord Rutland: We'll show those French what we English are made of.

Duke of Sussex: Aye. Verily, we will make a fine show. Have you seen the royal pavilion?

Lord Buckingham: Aye, that I have. Such splendour! Methinks 'twill dazzle French eyes.

Lord Rutland: Myself, I plan to spend much time practising at the barre and on the tourney field, so that I am in fine fettle for the games.

Lord Buckingham: *(Hastily)* Me, too.

Duke of Sussex: Me, too. The French had better watch out.

Lord Buckingham: This calls for a celebration. Let us go hunting and kill a deer. Or, even better, repair to the bear baiting. Anything that involves blood.

Lord Buckingham, **Lord Rutland** and the **Duke of Sussex**: *(Saluting with their swords)* Hurrah!

(Lights down on the three lords.)

Will: You see? They're thrilled.

Annie: Hmm. I wonder what their wives have to say about it?

SCENE 7

(Lady Buckingham, Lady Rutland, the Duchess of Sussex, Will, Annie)

A room in the Palace. Lights up on **Lady Buckingham, Lady Rutland** *and the* **Duchess of Sussex**. *They are embroidering.*

Lady Buckingham: So, Lady Rutland. Does your good husband accompany His Majesty to France?

Lady Rutland: *(Proudly)* Oh, yes. Naturally. He is quite a favourite with the King. What of *your* husband, Lady Buckingham?

Lady Buckingham: He goes also. I cannot say I shall greatly notice his absence; he is always off to the bear baiting … *(Putting her hands together)* But may the saints preserve him.

Duchess of Sussex: My Lord the Duke also attends. Our poor husbands. I fear for them. The voyage is most perilous.

Lady Rutland: I hear that ship's food leaves much to be desired. Let us pray they do not get scurvy. All one's teeth drop out, you know. So unpleasant.

Lady Buckingham: Well, we must just see that they take a sensible packed lunch.

Duchess of Sussex: No need, surely? His Majesty will not go short of provisions. The kitchens have been preparing for weeks.

Lady Rutland: *(Sighing)* I must say I wouldn't mind a trip to France. 'Twould make a change from endless needlework.

Lady Buckingham: Verily, I think 'tis more of a man thing. Travelling to foreign parts.

Lady Rutland: Mmm. You know what they say. All things have an end, and a pudding hath two.

*(**Lady Buckingham** and the **Duchess of Sussex** stare at her.)*

Lady Rutland: 'Tis a common Tudor saying.

Lady Buckingham: Meaning what, dear?

Lady Rutland: I haven't the faintest idea.

(They laugh merrily. Lights down.)

Will: Lady Rutland was right, though. The King – *(To the off-stage **Boys**)* Watch it! – will not go hungry. He will simply take food with him – and plenty of it.

Annie: He won't stint himself, that's for sure.

30

SCENE 8

(The Cook, Annie, Will, Humble Tom)

The Palace kitchen. Lights up on the **Cook**, *reading out a long list of provisions.*

Cook: *(Wearily)* Forty-two sheep, twenty-four pigs, two stags, thirty geese, two thousand pigeons, five hundred pheasants, fourteen swans, six cartloads of oysters and fish, one thousand five hundred eggs, four hundred pounds of butter. Should take care of breakfast. Now. On to lunch. *(Sighs)* Three hundred bitterns, nine hundred chickens …

(Lights down on the **Cook**.*)*

Annie: Will, I think I ought to mention something about this play.

Will: What about it?

Annie: Well, there have been a lot of historical facts and some quite interesting background stuff. And we've tried to capture the feel of the times.

Will: And you got in your stuff about the women's angle. *(To audience)* Bit *too* much of that, in my opinion.

Annie: But there's something missing.

Will: What?

Annie: A plot. And a character the audience can identify with. Someone with a story to tell. So far, it lacks drama.

Will: True. Who, though?

*(Enter **Humble Tom**, even dirtier. He trips over the twig.)*

Humble Tom: Ouch! *(To audience)* Here I be again. I'm retracing my steps because I've gone and lost my bundle.

Will and Annie: He'll do.

*(To **Humble Tom**'s surprise, he is gripped by the arms and propelled centre stage.)*

Will: There, lad. You have an audience. Tell your tale.

Humble Tom: Eh?

Will: Speak. Recount your story.

Humble Tom: Really? You're sure?

Annie: Just get on with it.

Humble Tom: Oh. Right. *(To audience)* Well, I'm Tom. Just a humble shepherd boy, up from the country. I've heard that His Majesty's off to France, and I'm on my way to London Town to join 'im! Well, that's what I'm hopin'. My Uncle Silas works at the Palace. I'm crossin' my fingers that he'll find me a job. 'Tis my dream to visit foreign parts …

SCENE 9

(Humble Tom, Tom's Mother, Tom's Father, Will, Annie)

*Flashback to a poor hovel in the country. From outside comes the sound of bleating sheep. **Tom's Mother** sits and spins. **Tom's Father** eats a bowl of pottage. Enter **Humble Tom**, hitting his head on the low lintel.*

Humble Tom: Ouch!

Tom's Mother: Ah, 'ere be Tom, back from 'erding the sheep. Will you have some supper, son?

Tom's Father: 'Tis pottage again. I wouldn't recommend it.

Humble Tom: Mother. Father. I've been thinking, while out on the lonely hills. I don't want to be a shepherd.

Tom's Father: Not be a *shepherd*? But the whole family are shepherds. We've been shepherds for hundreds of years. Your grandpappy, your Uncle Seth, your cousins, everyone. All we know is sheep.

Humble Tom: Aye. But I'm sick of sheep. I don't care if I never see another one. I have a mind to make something of myself. Travel the world. See a bit of life.

Tom's Mother: There's the village fayre on May Day. That's lively.

Humble Tom: Not lively enough. No, I'm determined to go to London Town. I shall make my way to Greenwich Palace, seek out Uncle Silas and find work with him. He works in the kitchens, right?

Tom's Father: *(Darkly)* Aye. Brother Silas, who ran away to be a cook. The black sheep of the family.

Tom's Mother: He made a lovely pottage, though. Very good with herbs.

Tom's Father: He turned his back on shepherdin'. That's it, as far as I be concerned. 'Tis bad luck to break with tradition.

Tom's Mother: Your dad's right. Oh, son, son! Don't go to London. There be the plague and the smallpox and the sweating sickness. You'll get boils.

Humble Tom: Well, I'm sorry, but I've made up my mind. Farewell, Mother. Farewell, Father. Wish me luck. I must say goodbye to the sheep. I haven't told them yet.

*(**Humble Tom** exits, hitting his head on the lintel again.)*

Humble Tom: Ouch!

Tom's Mother: *(Weeping)* Oh, Tom, Tom! Father, stop him!

Tom's Father: Too late, Mother. He's gone.

(From off-stage comes the pathetic sound of sheep bleating a fond farewell. Lights down on the humble hovel.)

Will: So young Tom set off to follow his dream. He tramped the muddy roads for long days and nights, falling into potholes, sleeping in haystacks …

Annie: Get a move on. They know about the appalling travelling conditions.

Will: … finally arriving in London …

Annie: We've seen that bit, too. Skip to the next bit.

*(**Humble Tom** joins them, tripping over the twig.)*

Humble Tom: Ouch! How did I do?

Will: Fine. I think you being so accident-prone has got their sympathy.

Annie: So, tell us. What happens next?

Humble Tom: I go to Greenwich.

Annie: Don't forget your bundle.

Humble Tom: Oh, right. Thanks.

*(Exit **Humble Tom**, with bundle. He trips over the twig again.)*

Humble Tom: Ouch!

SCENE 10

(**Humble Tom, Cutpurse Roger, Blind Olly, Dirty Christopher, Annie, Will**)

On the banks of the Thames at Greenwich. Lights up on **Humble Tom***.*

Humble Tom: Well, here I am at last, close to journey's end on the banks of the River Thames at Greenwich. I can't say it's been an easy journey, but at least it didn't involve sheep. I'll have a bite to eat, then make my way to the Palace kitchens.
*(**Humble Tom** rummages in his bundle. Enter **Cutpurse Roger**, **Blind Olly** and **Dirty Christopher**.)*

Cutpurse Roger: Oho! What 'ave we 'ere?

Blind Olly: Looks like an 'umble shepherd boy, up from the country.

Dirty Christopher: Let's rough 'im up an' steal 'is bundle.

Cutpurse Roger: And 'is crook.

Blind Olly: What do you want 'is crook for?

Dirty Christopher: I dunno. I'm strangely attracted to it, bein' a bit of a *crook* myself. Boom, boom!
*(They approach **Humble Tom** from behind. **Blind Olly** taps his shoulder.)*

Humble Tom: Ho there, good fellows all! 'Tis a
fine night … ow! What the …? Ooof! Ouch!
Get off me!

*(**Humble Tom** is set upon by **Cutpurse Roger**,
Blind Olly and **Dirty Christopher**. He is pushed
to the ground and relieved of his bundle and his
crook. Exit **Cutpurse Roger**, **Blind Olly** and
Dirty Christopher, laughing.)*

Humble Tom: Oh, *figs!*

*(Lights down on **Humble Tom**, in despair.)*

Annie: He's not having much luck, is he?

Will: No. Perhaps things will look up for him once he
reaches the Palace.

SCENE 11

(The Cook, Humble Tom, Will, Annie)

*The Palace kitchen. Lights up on the **Cook** and **Humble Tom**.*

Cook: So you're Brother Reuben's boy, eh?

Humble Tom: Aye, that I be, Uncle Silas.

Cook: And how are the sheep?

Humble Tom: Oh, you know. Woolly.

Cook: Aye. Get on your nerves, sheep.

Humble Tom: That they do. That's why I left and came to London Town.

Cook: After a bit of excitement, eh, young Tom? Want to see the entertainment? The shops? The hustle and bustle of the busy streets? The piles of festering rubbish?

Humble Tom: Well, yes. But mainly I was hoping to find work with you, here in the kitchens.

Cook: Well, I don't know about that. 'Tis all go. Tomorrow we depart for France.

SCENE 11

Humble Tom: What, for the Field of the Cloth of Gold? *(Fanfare)*

Cook: Well, that's what it becomes known as, aye.

Humble Tom: And you go too, Uncle?

Cook: Oh, aye. The King's not a great one for fancy French food. He likes his boiled mutton, three times a day.

Humble Tom: But this be the answer to my prayers! Oh, Uncle Silas! Take me with you! The sea calls to me. The roar of the surf, the wind in my hair ...

Cook: Ah, but can you cook?

Humble Tom: Not exactly. I can stir pottage.

Cook: Hah! Peasant food! Not fit for the likes of the gentry. Can you steam swan or bake bittern? Do you know the roasting time for mallard?

Humble Tom: No. I'm afraid not.

Cook: Well, it looks like you're out of luck, then, lad. Unless ...

Humble Tom: What?

Cook: Well, we're taking quite a lot of sheep.

Humble Tom: *(Sighing)* Oh, *figs.*

*(Lights down on **Humble Tom** and the **Cook**.)*

Will: Just can't get away from sheep, can he?

41

Annie: Still, at least he's going. He's going to get his big adventure. Unlike most of the women we've met. They're all staying at home, do you notice?

Will: That's Tudor life for you. The men have all the fun and the women stay at home. And that seems like a good place to end the play.

Annie: What, already? Time's up?

Will: Pretty much. I think they might need the hall for something else.

Annie: Well, *I* think we need an upbeat ending. Let's have one more scene. We'll set it at the port of Dover and get everyone on stage.

Will: And then what?

Annie: This is a play! It doesn't have to be one hundred per cent historically accurate. Rich, poor, young, old, men, women – we'll send every last one of them to the Field of the Cloth of Gold! *(Fanfare)*

SCENE 12

(The entire Cast)

The docks at Dover. To period music, the entire Cast (except Humble Tom) enter and take a bow, and then assemble on stage. The music fades.

Cast: We hope you have enjoyed our play,
And had a lot of fun,
But finally, we're sad to say,
Our story is now done.
We learned a lot of history,
And heard a simple tale,
But now the tide is turning,
And the wind is in the sail.
So hie you back to modern times,
Farewell to days of old,
But, as for us, *we're* sailing to …
… the Field of the Cloth of Gold!

Annie: Three cheers for the Tudors!

Will and Annie: Hip, hip!

Cast: Hurray!

Will and Annie: Hip, hip!

Cast: Hurray!

Will and Annie: Hip, hip!

Cast: Hurray!

*(Led by **Henry VIII** and talking amongst themselves, the **Cast** file off to mount the gangplank of a waiting ship.)*

Cast: Never been on a ship before ...

I hope the food's good ...

How does it stay up, d'you think?

Do they speak Spanish in France, or what?

Up the gangplank, Mother ...

Anyone heard the shipping forecast?

I'm feelin' queasy already ...

*(Enter **Humble Tom**, at a run.)*

Humble Tom: Stop! Come back! I've lost the sheep! Wait for me! Don't raise the gangplank ...

*(Too late. **Humble Tom** throws down his hat in frustration.)*

Humble Tom: Ah, *figs!*

*(Lights down on **Humble Tom**.)*

The End

About the play

The play is designed to be read in approximately 30 minutes. If you stage it for an audience it will take considerably longer, particularly if you are limited to one acting area.

This play is very tongue-in-cheek. Some children may find it quite a challenge; remember that comic timing is a real art!

Although the play is a spoof, it is set against an accurate historical backdrop. The meeting between Henry VIII and Francis really did take place – and Henry did wrestle Francis. (He lost!) There are references to the attitudes of the time; for example, the place of women in Tudor society. Characters step in and out of role, comment on the action, and at one point discuss the elements that make up a play. *Humble Tom's Big Trip* should be a springboard for some interesting discussions.

Staging

Keep it simple. There is no other way with a play that has so many changes of scene. Forget about scenery. The easiest way to set the play is to arrange for one of the actors to hold up a sign – *Henry's Chambers*, *Palace Kitchens*, etc. – at the beginning of each scene. If possible, use several acting areas to reduce the amount of time needed for scene changes. Scenes 5 and 12 require a large number of the cast to be on stage. The other scenes need six or fewer actors, so the acting areas can be relatively small. The narrators are present throughout. They can either move between acting areas or remain in one place.

Chairs are required from time to time. In addition, a few small props are needed: Tom's crook and bundle, a chamberpot, some embroidery, the street traders' wares and a list for the cook. Three swords are required for the noblemen. If you don't happen to have a lute for Henry, change it to a recorder. You will need to find some recorded Tudor-style music that can be faded in and out as required.

Costume

Most teachers will have neither the time nor the funds necessary to provide the cast with glorious, authentic Tudor outfits, so you will probably need to improvise. Study pictures of Tudor clothes with the children, and try to think of simple ways to achieve the "look". The easiest solution is to use basic undergarments – leotards and flowing skirts for the girls, plain t-shirts and leggings for the boys – and then to add one or two accessories. The clothes of the courtiers should be richly decorated. A flamboyant hat, a brightly coloured cloak or a lace head-dress will indicate nobility. Knickerbockers could be improvised from knickers stuffed with fabric and teamed with tights. There may be some long dresses that can be customised in your existing drama wardrobe. The common people are relatively easy to dress – basic tunics and leggings for the boys, and ragged skirts for the girls.

Remember – miracles can be achieved with crêpe paper and a stapler!

HODDER WAYLAND PLAYS

If you've enjoyed *Humble Tom's Big Trip*, try the other titles in the series:

Cruel Times by Kaye Umansky

Sissy is doing her best as a kitchen maid to earn the little money on which her Ma and family depend. But when she is robbed by a gang of urchins they face destitution – until she meets Charles Dickens. A tender-hearted story of rich and poor set in Queen Victoria's Britain.

Bombs and Blackberries by Julia Donaldson

Britain is at war, and the Chivers' youngest children have to leave their parents to live in the countryside. They are delighted to be brought back home when it looks as though the Germans aren't going to invade after all. But the air-raid siren goes off and this time it's frighteningly real... This dramatic and touching story is set in Manchester between 1939 and 1941.

The Head in the Sand by Julia Donaldson

Arthur Godbold digs up a bronze head from a Suffolk river. As he puzzles over it, the dramatic story of the Roman invasion of Britain unfolds in front of his very own eyes. Emperor Claudius, British Queen Boudicca, Roman soldiers and British slave girls are all involved in this fascinating and exciting story.

All these books can be purchased from your local bookseller. For more information about Hodder Wayland plays, write to:

The Sales Department, Hodder Children's Books,
A division of Hodder Headline Limited, 338 Euston Road,
London NW1 3BH